Food Truck Business Book for Beginners

How to Start, Finance & Market Your Business Step by Step

By Brian Mahoney

Disclaimer Notice

This book was written as a guide and for information, educational and entertainment purposes only. No warranties of any kind are expressed or implied.

Readers acknowledge that the author is not engaging in the rendering of legal, financial, medical or professional advice, and the information in this book is not meant to take the place of any professional advice. If advice is needed in any of these fields, you are advised to seek the services of a professional.

While the author has attempted to make the information in this book as accurate as possible, no guarantee is given as to the accuracy or currency of any individual item. Laws and procedures related to business, health and well being are constantly changing.

Therefore, in no event shall the author of this book be liable for any special, indirect, or consequential damages or any damages whatsoever in connection with the use of the information herein provided.

Table of Contents

Introduction

Starting a food truck business can offer numerous advantages, making it an appealing option for entrepreneurs in the food industry. Some of the key benefits include:

Lower initial investment: Compared to establishing a brick-and-mortar restaurant, setting up a food truck typically requires a lower initial investment, reducing the financial barrier to entry.

Flexibility and mobility: A food truck allows you to experiment with various locations and target different customer demographics, offering the flexibility to adjust your business strategy based on customer demand and popular events.

Lower operating costs: Operating costs such as rent and utilities are generally lower for a food truck than for a traditional restaurant. Additionally, staffing costs may be reduced, depending on the scale of the operation.

Wider reach and customer base: By strategically parking your food truck in high-traffic areas or near events, you can potentially reach a broader customer base, including office workers, event attendees, and pedestrians.

Innovation and creativity: Food trucks often provide an avenue for culinary innovation, allowing you to experiment with different cuisines and create unique, specialized menus that cater to specific tastes or dietary preferences.

Marketing and branding opportunities: A creatively designed food truck can serve as a moving advertisement for your brand. Building a strong social media presence can help you create a loyal customer base and keep them updated on your location and menu offerings.

Reduced risk: The lower overhead costs and initial investment, compared to a traditional restaurant, can mitigate the risks associated with starting a new business, providing a relatively safer entry point into the food industry.

Rapid feedback and adaptation: Direct interaction with customers can provide immediate feedback on your offerings, allowing you to make quick adjustments to your menu and business model, fostering better customer satisfaction and loyalty.

Entry into the food industry: For aspiring restaurateurs or chefs, a food truck can serve as an entry point into the food industry, providing valuable experience in managing a food business without the high costs and risks associated with a full-fledged restaurant.

While these benefits make the food truck business an attractive option, it is important to consider the challenges, such as local regulations, competition, and seasonality, when planning and executing a successful food truck venture.

BURRITOS
AZTECA
TACOS
AZ   C

Chapter 1
Getting Started in Business Step by Step

Getting Started in Business

There are over thirty million home-based businesses in the United States alone.

Many people dream of the independence and financial reward of having a home business. Unfortunately they let analysis paralysis stop them from taking action. This chapter is designed to give you a road map to get started. The most difficult step in any journey is the first step.

Anthony Robbins created a program called Personal Power. I studied the program a long time ago, and today I would summarize it, by saying you must figure out a way to motivate yourself to take massive action without fear of failure.

2 Timothy 1:7 King James Version

"For God hath not given us the spirit of fear; but of power, and of love, and of a sound mind."

Getting Started in Business

STEP #1 MAKE AN OFFICE IN YOUR HOUSE

If you are serious about making money, then redo the man cave or the woman's cave and make a place for you to do business, uninterupted.

STEP #2 BUDGET OUT TIME FOR YOU BUSINESS

If you already have a job, or if you have children, then they can take up a great deal of your time. Not to mention well meaning friends who use the phone to become time theives. Budget time for your business and stick to it.

STEP #3 DECIDE ON THE TYPE OF BUSINESS

You don't have to be rigid, but begin with the end in mine. You can become more flexible as you gain experience.

STEP #4 LEGAL FORM FOR YOUR BUSINESS

The three basic legal forms are sole proprietorship, partnership, and corporation. Each one has it's advantages. Go to www.Sba.gov and learn about each and make a decision.

STEP #5 PICK A BUSINESS NAME AND REGISTER IT

One of the safest ways to pick a business name is to use your own name. Your own name is not copywrited.

However, always check with an Attorney or the proper legal authority when dealing with legal matters.

STEP #6 WRITE A BUSINESS PLAN

This would seem like a no brainer. No matter what you are trying to accomplish you should have a blueprint. You should have a business plan. In the NFL about seven headcoaches get fired every season. So in a very competetive business, a man with no head coaching experience got hired by the NFL's Philadelphia Eagles. His name was Andy Reid. Andy Reid would later become the most successful coach in the team's history. One of the reasons the owner hired him, was because he had a business plan the size of a telephone book. Your business plan does not need to be nearly that big, but if you plan for as much as possible, you are less likely to get rattled when things don't go as planned.

STEP #7 PROPER LICENSES & PERMITS

Go to city hall and find out what you need to do, to start a home business.

STEP #8 SELECT BUSINESS CARDS, STATIONERY, BROCHURES

This is one of the least expensive ways to not only start your business but to promote and network your business.

STEP #9 OPEN A BUSINESS CHECKING ACCOUNT

Having a separate business account makes it much easier to keep track of profit and expenses. This will come in very handy, whether you decide to do your own taxes or hire out an professional.

STEP #10 TAKE SOME SORT OF ACTION TODAY!

This is not meant to be a comprehensive plan to start a business. It is meant to point you in the right direction to get started. You can go to the Small Business Administration for many free resources for starting your business. They even have a program(SCORE) that will give you access to many retired professionals who will advise you for free!
www.score.org

MILANESE ICE CREAM
99Flake

Chapter 2
Understanding the Food Truck Industry

Evolution of the Food Truck Industry and its Current Trends:

The food truck industry has experienced a remarkable transformation over the past few decades. What was once primarily associated with basic street foods and quick snacks has evolved into a sophisticated culinary experience, showcasing diverse cuisines and gourmet dishes.

a. Rise of Gourmet Offerings: One of the significant shifts in the industry has been the rise of gourmet food trucks, offering high-quality, specialized, and innovative cuisines, often at relatively affordable prices.

b. Fusion and Unique Concepts: Food trucks have embraced the trend of fusion foods, blending different culinary traditions to create unique offerings. This trend has attracted a diverse customer base and has been instrumental in driving the industry forward.

c. Emphasis on Health and Dietary Preferences: With the increasing focus on health and dietary preferences, many food trucks now offer options catering to specific dietary requirements, such as vegan, gluten-free, and organic food options, appealing to a health-conscious customer base.

d. Technological Integration: Many successful food truck businesses have integrated technology into their operations, leveraging social media platforms and mobile apps to enhance their visibility, engage with customers, and streamline the ordering process.

Analysis of the Target Market and Customer Preferences:

a. Urban Dwellers: Food trucks primarily target urban areas with high foot traffic, catering to a diverse demographic of office workers, students, tourists, and locals looking for a quick and convenient dining experience.

b. Millennial and Gen Z Customers: These demographics often seek unique culinary experiences and are open to trying new and innovative dishes, making them a significant target market for food truck businesses.

c. Health-Conscious Consumers: With the rising health consciousness, food trucks that offer healthier menu options or cater to specific dietary preferences have gained popularity among customers seeking nutritious yet convenient meal options.

d. Budget-Conscious Consumers: The affordability of food truck offerings compared to traditional restaurants appeals to budget-conscious consumers, making food trucks an attractive dining option.

Exploration of Successful Food Truck Businesses and Their Strategies:

a. Leveraging Social Media: Successful food truck businesses actively use social media platforms to promote their offerings, engage with customers, and announce their location and menu, creating a strong online presence.

b. Consistent Quality and Innovation: Food trucks that maintain consistent quality in their offerings while regularly introducing innovative menu items tend to attract and retain a loyal customer base.

c. Strategic Location Selection: Identifying and targeting locations with high foot traffic, such as business districts, universities, and popular tourist spots, contributes significantly to the success of a food truck business.

d. Customer Engagement and Experience: Food truck businesses that prioritize customer engagement, provide excellent service, and create a memorable dining experience often enjoy increased customer loyalty and positive word-of-mouth marketing.

e. Efficient Operations and Adaptability: Successful food truck businesses optimize their operations to ensure quick service without compromising on food quality. Additionally, they demonstrate adaptability by responding to changing customer preferences and market trends.

The food truck industry continues to evolve, catering to the dynamic preferences of consumers and leveraging technology to expand their reach. Successful businesses in this industry understand the importance of offering diverse, high-quality menu options, prioritizing customer experience, and adapting to the changing culinary landscape.

Food Truck

Chapter 3
Designing and Equipping Your Food Truck

Choosing the right food truck model, customizing the interior layout, and selecting high-quality equipment and appliances are crucial steps for running a successful food truck business. Here's a comprehensive guide to help you navigate through each of these steps:

Choosing the right food truck model:

a. Size and layout: Consider the type of cuisine you will be serving and the equipment you will need. A larger truck allows for more equipment and a broader menu but may have higher operational costs. Make sure the model you choose can accommodate all necessary appliances and storage while still providing enough space for your staff to work efficiently.

b. Mobility and durability: Opt for a model that is sturdy and has good mobility. Look for features such as good suspension, reliable tires, and a strong engine. It should also be easy to maneuver in different terrains and weather conditions.

Customizing the interior layout for optimal efficiency and functionality:

a. Workflow optimization: Design the layout in a way that optimizes the workflow, from food preparation to serving customers. Consider the logical flow of ingredients, cooking, assembly, and service. Make sure the layout enables smooth movement for your staff to avoid congestion and maximize productivity.

b. Ergonomics and safety: Prioritize the safety and comfort of your staff. Ensure that the layout allows for easy access to equipment and minimizes hazards. Incorporate non-slip flooring, fire-resistant materials, and proper ventilation to create a safe and healthy working environment.

Selecting high-quality equipment and appliances within budget constraints:

a. Prioritize essential equipment: Invest in high-quality essentials such as grills, deep fryers, refrigerators, and storage units. Look for appliances that are durable, energy-efficient, and easy to maintain. Choose equipment that aligns with your menu and cooking requirements.

b. Consider multi-functional appliances: To optimize space and reduce costs, select appliances that can perform multiple functions. For instance, a combination oven can serve as both a convection oven and a steamer, saving space and costs compared to having separate units for each function.

c. Research reputable brands and suppliers: Read reviews, consult industry experts, and consider the reputation of brands and suppliers before making a purchase. Compare prices and features to find the best value for your budget without compromising on quality and reliability.

d. Plan for maintenance and repairs: Factor in the costs of regular maintenance and repairs when budgeting for equipment. Choose equipment with readily available spare parts and a reliable warranty to minimize downtime and unexpected expenses.

By carefully considering these factors, you can set up a food truck that is not only efficient and functional but also well-equipped to meet your business needs within your budget constraints.

Here are ten popular food truck supply websites:

WebstaurantStore

URL: https://www.webstaurantstore.com/

Summary: WebstaurantStore is a leading online supplier of restaurant equipment and supplies, offering a wide range of products including kitchen supplies, cooking equipment, and food truck essentials.

FoodTruckEmpire.com

URL: https://foodtruckempire.com/

Summary: FoodTruckEmpire.com is a comprehensive resource for aspiring food truck owners. While not strictly a supply website, it provides valuable information on how to start and run a successful food truck business, including advice on where to source supplies.

RestaurantSupply.com

URL: https://www.restaurantsupply.com/

Summary: RestaurantSupply.com is an online restaurant supply store that caters to a variety of businesses, including food trucks. It offers a wide range of products such as commercial kitchen equipment, food prep tools, and restaurant furniture.

KaTom Restaurant Supply

URL: https://www.katom.com/

Summary: KaTom is a renowned restaurant supply company that offers a diverse range of products, including items suitable for food trucks. They provide commercial kitchen equipment, food prep tools, and more.

Food Truck Parts & Equipment

URL: https://www.foodtruckparts.net/
Summary: Food Truck Parts & Equipment specializes in providing specific parts and equipment tailored for food trucks. They offer a variety of products including food truck appliances, hardware, and accessories.

FoodTruckPartsDepot.com

URL: https://www.foodtruckpartsdepot.com/

Summary: FoodTruckPartsDepot.com is a one-stop-shop for various parts and components specifically designed for food trucks. They provide a range of products such as cooking equipment, refrigeration units, and truck accessories.

AcityDiscount

URL: https://www.acitydiscount.com/

Summary: ACityDiscount is a supplier of new and used commercial kitchen equipment suitable for food trucks. They offer a wide range of products including cooking appliances, refrigeration units, and food prep tools.

FoodTruckEquipment.com

URL: https://www.foodtruckequipment.com/

Summary: FoodTruckEquipment.com is a specialized supplier of equipment and supplies tailored to the needs of food truck operators. They offer a variety of products such as cooking equipment, storage solutions, and truck accessories.

Restaurant Equippers

URL: https://www.equippers.com/
Summary: Restaurant Equippers is a supplier of a wide range of restaurant equipment, including items suitable for food trucks. They provide commercial-grade products such as cooking appliances, refrigeration units, and food preparation tools.

Central Restaurant Products

URL: https://www.centralrestaurant.com/
Summary: Central Restaurant Products is a leading supplier of restaurant equipment and supplies, catering to various businesses including food trucks. They offer an extensive range of products such as kitchen appliances, cookware, and food storage solutions.

Chapter 4
Best Way To Write A Business Plan

How to Write a Business Plan

Millions of people want to know what is the secret to making money. Most have come to the conclusion that it is to start a business. So how to start a business? The first thing you do to start is business is to create a business plan.

A business plan is a formal statement of a set of business goals, the reasons they are believed attainable, and the plan for reaching those goals. It may also contain background information about the organization or team attempting to reach those goals.

A professional business plan consists of eight parts.

1. Executive Summary

The executive summary is a very important part of your business plan. Many consider it the most important because it this part of your plan gives a summary of the current state of your business, where you want to take it and why the business plan you have made will be a success. When requesting funds to start your business, the executive summary is an chance to get the attention of a possible investor.

How to Write a Business Plan

2. Company Description

The company description part of your business plan gives a high level review of the different aspects of your business. This is like putting your elevator pitch into a brief summary that can help readers and possible investors quickly grasp the goal of your business and what will make it stand out, or what unique need it will fill.

3. Market Analysis

The market analysis part of your business plan should go into detail about your industries market and monetary potential. You should demonstrate detailed research with logical strategies for market penetration. Will you use low prices or high quality to penetrate the market?

4. Organization and Management

The Organization and Management section follows the Market Analysis. This part of the business plan will have your companies organizational structure, the type of business structure of incorporation, the ownership, management team and the qualifications of everyone holding these positions including the board of directors if necessary.

How to Write a Business Plan

5. Service or Product Line

The Service or Product Line part of your business plan gives you a chance to describe your service or product. Focus on the benefits to the customers more than what the product or service does. For example, a air conditioner makes cold air. The benefit of the product is it cools down and makes customers more comfortable whether they are driving in bumper to bumper traffic or a sick and sitting in a nursing home. Air Conditioners fill a need that could mean the difference between life and death. Use this section to state what are the most important benefits of your product or service and what need it fills.

6. Marketing and Sales

Having a proven marketing plan is essential element to the success of any business. Today online sales are dominating the marketplace. Present a strong internet marketing plan as well as social media plan. YouTube videos, Facebook Ads and Press Releases all can be part of your internet marketing plan. Passing out foyers and business cards are still an effective way to reach potential customers.

Use this part of your business plan to state your projected sales and how you came to that number. Do your research on similar companies for possible statistics on sales numbers.

How to Write a Business Plan

7. Funding Request

When you write your Funding Request section of your business plan, be sure to be detailed and have documentation of the cost of supplies, building space, transportation, overhead and promotion of your business.

8. Financial Projections

The following is a list of the important financial statements to include in your business plan packet.

Historical Financial Data

Your historical financial data would be bank statements, balance sheets and possible collateral for your loan.

Prospective Financial Data

The prospective financial data section of your business plan should show you potential growth within your industry, projecting out for at least the next five years.

You can have monthly or quarterly projections for the first year. Then project from year to year.

Include a ratio and trend analysis for all of your financial statements. Use colorful graphs to explain positive trends, as part of the financial projections section of your business plan.

How to Write a Business Plan

Appendix

The appendix should not be part of the main body of your business plan. It should only be provided on a need to know basis. Your business plan may be seen by a lot of people and you don't want certain information available to everybody. Lenders may need such information so you should have an appendix ready just in case.

The appendix would include:

Credit history (personal & business)

 Resumes of key managers

 Product pictures

 Letters of reference

 Details of market studies

 Relevant magazine articles or book references

 Licenses, permits or patents

 Legal documents

 Copies of leases

How to Write a Business Plan

Building permits

Contracts

List of business consultants, including attorney and accountant

Keep a record of who you allow to see your business plan.

Include a Private Placement Disclaimer. A Private Placement Disclaimers is a private placement memorandum (PPM) is a document focused mainly on the possible downsides of an investment.

Chapter 5
Crowd Funding

Crowd Funding Crowd Sourcing

In 2015 over $34 billion dollars was raised by crowdfunding. Crowdfunding and Crowdsourcing roots began in 2005 and they help to finance or fund projects by raising money from a large number of people, usually by using the internet.

This type of fundraising or venture capital usually has 3 components. The individual or organization with a project that needs funding, groups of people who donate to the project, and a organization sets up a structure or rules to put the tow together.

These websites do charge fees. The standard fee for success is about %5. If your goal is not met there is also a fee.

Below is a list of the top Crowdfunding websites according to myself and Entrepreneur Magazine Contributor Sally Outlaw.

Crowd Funding Crowd Sourcing

https://www.indiegogo.com/

Started as a platform for getting movies made, now helps to raise funds any cause.

http://rockethub.com/

Started as a platform for the arts, now it helps to raise funds for business, science, social projects and education.

http://peerbackers.com/

Peerbackers focuses on raising funds for business, entrepreneurs and innovators.

https://www.kickstarter.com/

The most popular and well know n of all the crowdfunding websites. Kickstarter focuses on film, music, technology, gaming, design and the creative arts. Kickstarter only accepts projects from the United States, Canada and the United Kingdom.

Crowd Funding Crowd Sourcing

http://group.growvc.com/

This website is for business and technology innovation.

https://microventures.com/

Get access to angel investors. This website is for business startups.

https://angel.co/

Another website for business startups.

https://circleup.com/

Circle up is for innovative consumer companies.

https://www.patreon.com/

If you start a YouTube Channel (highly recommended) you will hear about this website frequently. This website if for creative content people.

Crowd Funding Crowd Sourcing

https://www.crowdrise.com/

"Raise money for any cause that inspires you."
Landing page slogan speaks for itself. #1 fundraising
website for personal causes.

https://www.gofundme.com/

This fundraising website allows for business, charity,
education, emergencies, sports, medical, memorials,
animals, faith, family, newlyweds etc...

https://www.youcaring.com/

The leader in free fundraising. Over $400 million
raised.

https://fundrazr.com/

"FundRazr is laser-focused on eliminating the
guesswork of raising money online for your
campaign. Our technology and social media guidance
make telling your powerful story easy; sharing it with
the widest community simple; and collecting the
money worry-free. "

Chapter 6
$5 Million Dollars to Fund Your Business

$5 Million Dollars to Fund Your Business

Loans guaranteed by the Small Business Administration can be as little as $500 to as big as $5 Million Dollars!

The money can be used for a variety of business needs, including the purchase of long-term fixed assets and for operating expenses. Some loan programs do have restrictions on how the loan money can be used, so you will have to check with a Small Business Administration approved lender when looking for a loan. The lender can match you with the correct loan for your business needs.

Working capital

Like seasonal financing, export loans, revolving credit, and refinanced business debt.

Fixed assets

Like office equipment, property, tools, machinery, business equipment, construction, and remodeling.

$5 Million Dollars to Fund Your Business

Eligibility requirements

Lenders and loan programs have distinctive eligibility guide lines. Basically, eligibility is related to what a business does to receive its funding, the character of its ownership, and location of the businesses operation. Usually, businesses must meet size standards.

What is a small business size standard?

A size standard, under most circumstances is stated in number of employees or average yearly receipts, and represents the biggest size that a business (including its subsidiaries and affiliates) may be to remain classified as a small business for Small Business Administration and government contracting programs. The definition of "small" can be different in different industries.

How to calculate your small business size

Size standards are mostly based on the average annual receipts or the average number of employees.

$5 Million Dollars to Fund Your Business

Eligibility requirements

You must be able to repay the loan. You must have a credible business objective. Individuals with bad credit may still qualify for business startup money. Lenders will give you a list of the lending guide lines and requirements for your loan. Here are a few more.

Be a for-profit business

The business is properly registered and performs as a legal business.

Do business in the U.S.

The business is physically located and operates in the United States and or its territories.

You Have invested equity

You the business owner has invested your own time or finances into the business.

$5 Million Dollars to Fund Your Business

Eligibility requirements

Exhaust financing options

The business cannot get money from any other financial lender.

Loans for exporters

Most United States banks view loans for exporters as risky. This can make it more difficult for you to get loans for things like day-to-day operations, advance orders with suppliers, and debt refinancing. That's why the Small Business Administration came up with programs to make it easier for United States small businesses to get loans for an export business.

To learn how the SBA can help you get an export loan, contact your local Small Business Administration International Trade Finance Specialist or the Small Business Administration's Office of International Trade.

https://www.sba.gov/funding-programs/loans

Chapter 7
How to set up a LLC

How to set up a LLC

Starting up a Limited Liability Company (LLC) has many steps, which include selecting a business name, filing the required paperwork with the proper government agency, and fulfilling any additional obligations in your state. Here's a basic overview of the process:

Select a Name for Your LLC:

Your LLC's name must be unique and different from other businesses in your state.

It usually must have the words "Limited Liability Company" or abbreviations like "LLC" or "L.L.C."

Select a Registered Agent:

Select a registered agent who is responsible for legal documents on behalf of the corporation. This can be one person or a registered agent service.

Submit Articles of Organization:

Submit the Articles of Organization (also refered as the Certificate of Formation or similar) with the Secretary of State or the required state agency. Each state has its own form, and you can usually submit them online or by mail.

Pay the filing fee, which are different from state to state.

How to set up a LLC

Get a Operating Agreement:

While not always required by law, it's strongly recommended to create an Operating Agreement that outlines the ownership structure, management, and operating procedures of the LLC. This document is not typically filed with the state but is essential for internal governance.

Get a Employer Identification Number (EIN):

An EIN, also referred as a Federal Tax Identification Number, is a necessary for tax requirement. Contact the IRS by mail, online or a local office to apply for one, usually at no cost.

Comply with State and Local obligations:

Contact your state and local government to see if there are any additional obligations or licenses needed to operate your LLC legally. This may include business licenses, permits, and zoning approvals.

Pay State Fees and Taxes:

Your LLC may be subject to state filing fees and yearly taxes. Ensure you meet all financial obligations to maintain your LLC's good standing.

How to set up a LLC

File yearly Reports:

Some states ask LLCs to file yearly reports to provide updated information about the business and pay any associated fees.

Open a Business Bank Account:

To keep your personal and business finances separate, open a business bank account specifically for your LLC.

Observe Ongoing Compliance:

Be aware of ongoing compliance obligations, including filing yearly reports, paying taxes, and renewing licenses and permits.

Seek Advice from Attorneys and Business experts:

You should seek advice from legal and financial professionals or a business attorney who can help you navigate the legal and tax aspects specific to your situation.

Forming a LLC can give you and your business needed legal protection. Make sure to contact the proper authorities in your state to take advantage of all that a LLC has to offer.

Chapter 8
Business Insurance

BUSINESS INSURANCE

Consult an attorney for any and all of your business matters.

In the early 1990's an elderly woman purchased a hot cup of coffee from a McDonald's drive-thru window in Albuquerque. She spilled the coffee, and suffered 3rd degree burns. She sued Mcdonald's and won. She won 2.7 million dollars in a punitive damages victory. The verdict was appealed and settlement is estimated at somewhere in the neighborhood of $500,000 dollars. All because she spilled the coffee into her lap, while trying to add sugar and cream.

Two men in Ohio, were carpet layers. They were severely burned when a three and a half gallon container of carpet adhesive ignited, when the hot water heater it was sitting next to, was turned on. They felt the warning lable on the back of the can was insufficient. So they filed a lawsuit against the adhesive manufacturers and were awarded nine million dollars.

A woman in Oklahoma, purchased a brad new Winnebago. While driving it home, she set the cruise control to 70 miles per hour. She then left the drivers seat to make some coffee or a sandwich in the back of the motor home.

BUSINESS INSURANCE

The vehicle crashed and the woman sued Winnebago for not advising her, that cruise control does not drive and steer the vehicle. She won 1.7 million dollars and the company had to rewrite their instruction manual.

Unfortunately all three outrageous lawsuits are real. If you are going to run a business, any business, you should consider protecting yourself with Professional Liability Insurance, also known as Errors and Omissions (E & 0) insurance.

This type of insurance can help to protect you from having to pay the full cost of defending yourself against a negligence lawsuit claim.

Error and Omissions can protect you against claims that are not usually covered in regular liability insurance. Those policies usually cover bodily harm, or damage to property. Error and Omissions can protect you agaist negligence, and other mental anguish like inaccurate advice, or misrepresentation. Criminal prosecution is not covered.

Errors and Ommision insurance is recommended for notaries public, real estate brokers or investors and professionals like: software engineers, lawyers, home inspectors web site delvelopers and landscape architects to name a few professions.

BUSINESS INSURANCE

The Most Common Errors and Omission Claims:

%25 Breach of Fiduciary Duty

%15 Breach of Contract

%14 Negligence

%13 Failure to Supervise

%11 Unsuitability

%10 Other

BUSINESS INSURANCE

Things you should know about or require before purchasing a Errors and Omission policy is...

* What is the limit of liability

* What is the Deductible

* Does it include FDD First Dollar Defense - which obligates the insurance company to fight a case without a deductible first.

* Do I have Tail-end coverage or Extended Reporting Coverage (insurance that lasts into retirement)

* Extended coverage for Employees

* Cyber Liability Coverage

* Department of Labor Fiduciary Coverage

* Insolvency Coverage

If you get Errors and Omission insurance, renew it the day it expires. You must be careful to avoid gaps in your coverage, or it could result in not getting your policy renewed.

BUSINESS INSURANCE

A few E & O Insurance Providers:

Insureon

Insureon states that their median Errors and Omissions Insurance policy cost about $750 a year or about $65 a month. The price of course will vary according to your business, the policy you choose and other risk factors.

https://www.insureon.com/home

EOforless

EOforless.com helps insurance, investment, and real estate professionals buy E & O insurance at an affordable cost in five minutes or less.

https://www.eoforless.com/

BUSINESS INSURANCE

CalSurance Associates

As a leading insurance broker, CalSurance Associates, a division of Brown & Brown Program Insurance Services, Inc. has over fifty years of experience delivering comprehensive insurance products, exceptional service, and proven results to over 150,000 insured. They serve professionals nationwide and across multiple industries, including some of the largest financial firms and insurance companies in the United States.

http://www.calsurance.com/csweb/index.aspx

Better Safe Than Sorry

Insurance is one of the hidden costs of doing business. These are just a few companies and a brief overview on the topic of business insurance. Make sure to talk to an attorney or quailified insurance agent before making any decision on insurance. Protece you and your business. Many states do not require E & O insurances. But when you see the cost of some of the settlements, it's better to be safe than sorry.

→ STILL WATER - 1€50
→ SPARKLING WATER - 1€50
→ COKE - 2€
→ WATER
WE H
W

Chapter 9
Marketing Your Food Truck Business

Marketing your food truck business effectively can significantly contribute to its success. Here are some key strategies to consider:

Define your brand: Develop a strong brand identity that sets you apart from competitors. This includes your truck's name, logo, color scheme, and overall theme.

Social media presence: Utilize platforms like Instagram, Facebook, and Twitter to share enticing images of your food, updates on locations, and behind-the-scenes glimpses. Engage with your followers by responding to comments and messages promptly.

Location-based marketing: Use location-based apps like Google Maps, Yelp, and Foursquare to make it easier for customers to find you. Regularly update your current location to keep your customers informed.

Collaborations and partnerships: Collaborate with local businesses, events, or organizations to widen your customer base. Participating in local food festivals or community events can also help you gain exposure.

Loyalty programs and promotions: Offer incentives like loyalty cards, discounts, or special promotions for repeat customers. Encourage customers to follow your social media accounts or sign up for a newsletter to receive exclusive deals and updates.

Eye-catching design: Invest in a visually appealing truck design that reflects your brand and makes a lasting impression on potential customers. A well-designed truck can attract attention and generate interest in your food offerings.

Online ordering and delivery: Set up an online ordering system or partner with food delivery services to reach customers who prefer the convenience of ordering from home or the office.

Customer feedback and reviews: Encourage customers to leave reviews and feedback on platforms like Yelp or Google. Positive reviews can enhance your credibility and attract new customers.

Sampling and tastings: Offer free samples or tastings at local events or high-traffic areas. This can entice people to try your food, potentially leading to new customers.

Email marketing: Collect customer emails through your website or at the point of sale and send out regular newsletters or updates about your menu, promotions, and upcoming events.

Engage with the local community: Participate in local charity events, fundraisers, or community gatherings. Building a positive reputation within the community can help you establish a loyal customer base.

Consistent quality and service: Maintain consistent food quality and excellent customer service to ensure that customers have a positive experience and are more likely to return and recommend your food truck to others.

By combining these strategies, you can create a comprehensive marketing plan that helps promote your food truck business and increase its visibility and customer base.

Conclusion

In Chapter 1, you learned the initial steps and considerations for starting a food truck business, following a step-by-step guide to entrepreneurship.

In Chapter 2, you discovered insights into the food truck industry, gaining knowledge about its unique trends, challenges, and opportunities.

In Chapter 3, you learned about the practical aspects of setting up a food truck, including design and equipment considerations crucial for efficient food service.

In Chapter 4, you gained insights into the best practices for writing a comprehensive business plan, which is essential for attracting investors and guiding your food truck venture.

In Chapter 5, you explored the concept of crowdfunding as a potential source of capital for your food truck business, understanding strategies for a successful campaign.

In Chapter 6, you learned about various funding options, including the possibility of securing a substantial amount of capital, perhaps as much as $5 million, to fund your food truck business.

In Chapter 7, you discovered the process of setting up a Limited Liability Company (LLC), understanding its importance as a legal structure for small businesses.

In Chapter 8, you delved into the significance of business insurance for your food truck, learning about different coverage types to protect your business and assets effectively.

In Chapter 9, you gained insights into various marketing strategies tailored specifically for food truck businesses, including the use of social media, branding, and other promotional techniques to attract customers.

Now you have a sound foundation for starting a food truck business. But to take your dream to a reality you must take action.

"You don't have to be great to start. But you have to start to be great." Zig Ziglar

Food Truck Business Resources

Starting a food truck business can be an exciting venture. Here are some recommended resources for further reading and research as well as a directory of industry-specific organizations and regulatory bodies:

Books:

"The Food Truck Handbook: Start, Grow, and Succeed in the Mobile Food Business"
by David Weber.

"The Complete Idiot's Guide to Starting a Food Truck Business" by Alan Philips.

"Running a Food Truck For Dummies" by Richard Myrick.

"Start Your Own Food Truck Business: Cart, Trailer, Kiosk, Standard and Gourmet Trucks, Mobile Catering and Bustaurant" by The Staff of Entrepreneur Media.

Websites and Blogs:

Mobile-Cuisine.com: Offers news, resources, and information for the mobile food industry.

FoodTruckr.com: Provides tips, strategies, and advice for starting and running a successful food truck business.

Magazines and Publications:

Food Truck Operator: Provides information, news, and insights specific to the food truck industry.

Mobile Food & Beverage Magazine: Offers insights into the mobile food and beverage industry, including trends, best practices, and success stories.

Industry-Specific Organizations:

National Food Truck Association (NFTA): Represents the food truck industry's interests and provides resources for food truck owners and operators.

The Institute of Food Technologists (IFT): Offers resources and information related to food science and technology, which can be beneficial for understanding food safety and regulations.

The U.S. Small Business Administration (SBA): Provides resources and support for small businesses, including those in the food industry.

Regulatory Bodies:

U.S. Food and Drug Administration (FDA): Provides information on regulations and guidelines for food safety and handling.

Department of Health and Human Services: Offers information on health and safety regulations that apply to food service businesses.

Local Health Departments: Check your local health department's website for specific regulations and permits required for operating a food truck in your area.

These resources should provide a good starting point for your research and help you navigate the complexities of starting a food truck business. Always ensure to stay updated with the latest regulations and industry trends to stay competitive and compliant.

We want to thank you for the purchase of this book and more importantly, thank you for reading it to the end. We hope your reading experience was pleasurable and that you would inform your family and friends on your favorite social media.

We would like to continue to provide you with high-quality books, and that end, would you mind leaving us a review if at all possible.

We are extremely grateful for your assistance.

Warm Regards,
Brian Mahoney
CEO
MahoneyProducts Publishing